NORFOLK POST OFFICES

THEN and NOW

Barrie King

Photography
by Roger Griffiths

JOHN NICKALLS PUBLICATIONS

DEDICATION

Dedicated to my late wife Una,
my son Stephen, my daughter Lindsay
and my step-daughter Lesley Anne

PREVIOUS TITLE BY THE AUTHOR
North Norfolk, A Portrait in Old Picture Postcards

First published in 2009 by John Nickalls Publications
Oak Farm Bungalow, Sawyers Lane, Suton
Wymondham, Norfolk, NR18 9SH
Telephone/Fax: 01953 601893

ISBN 978 1 904136 30 9

Designed by Ashley Gray

Printed by The Complete Product Company Limited
Unit 20a, Diss Business Park, Hopper Way, Sandy Lane
Diss, Norfolk IP22 4GT

CONTENTS

ACKNOWLEDGEMENTS

I would like to thank my partner Christine for all her help and patience during the research carried out for this book, her knowledge of shorthand was invaluable. My thanks must also go to fellow postcard collector Gerald Lamont (Fakenham) for allowing me to use postcards from his own collection along with his knowledge of North Norfolk. I must also thank most sincerely Roger Griffiths (Fakenham) for his brilliant photographic work and the dangers he had to endure when standing in the middle of main roads to acquire the right position for taking the pictures.

I would also like to thank all the people who gave me information on the various buildings that used to be post offices, many of which are now private dwellings. Some of these premises are still occupied by generations of the same family and a few are still post offices today. Please accept my apologies for anyone that I have unintentionally forgotten and any errors made.

ABOUT THE AUTHOR

Barrie King was born in Fakenham, Norfolk, and, apart from ten years working in Suffolk, has lived there all his life.

Most of his working life has been in the printing industry in Fakenham. His main hobbies are playing golf and collecting postcards, mainly of Fakenham, surrounding villages and Norfolk post offices.

Barrie's first book was *North Norfolk, A Portrait in Old Picture Postcards*, which was published in 2002.

ABOUT THE PHOTOGRAPHER

Roger Griffiths was born in 1950 and has lived in Norfolk since 1987.

He was in the RAF for twenty-six years and, after leaving the RAF, he took a position with an international computer company which, over the years, has taken him to most parts of the world.

Roger has been interested in photography from a very early age. Much of the work he undertakes now is for weddings, portraits, landscapes, advertising and commercial photography.

INTRODUCTION

It is not too many years ago that every village had its own post office, however, like railways and railway stations, most of them have been closed. In some villages the post office carried on for a short time in the local village hall, private dwellings or even in adjoining garages. The closure of so many post offices is extremely sad as in most communities it was the hub of the village where people not only frequented the premises for stamps, pensions or to post parcels and letters etc, but to meet up with friends and acquaintances and of course discuss the latest local news and happenings.

The post office counter has gone from a flat polished mahogany top, with easy contact and access between the postmaster or postmistress, to a glass screen and, although it proves quite difficult to hold conversation through these screens, sadly they are a sign of the times for security purposes.

The first picture postcards were published in 1894 and were known as 'court cards'. They were a lot smaller in size compared with today's cards. Court cards had space for a message on one side with the address being on the reverse side.

In 1902 the size was increased and they were printed with a dividing line down the centre of the back, these were referred to as a 'divided back'. The message was written on the left-hand side of the dividing line and the address on the right-hand side, with a picture on the front. This type of card is still in use today.

Finally, with the many letters of appreciation I received regarding my first book, *North Norfolk, A Portrait in Old Picture Postcards*, I trust that this second publication of *Norfolk Post Offices – Then and Now* will give as much pleasure to those who read it.

Barrie King
Fakenham, 2009

FRONT COVER: *Top left*: Wells Road Post Office *c.* 1971; *Bottom right*: Demolishing the old Post Office after completion of a new one in the background. ABBREVIATIONS: *c.* (circa) – approximately; *p.u.* – postally used.

THEN – AYLSHAM POST OFFICE, *c.* **1914:** The post office was in this building from 1st January, 1893. One of the earliest recorded post-masters was Mr Harcourt Augustus McCreedy, 1904. The soldiers seen lined up in this postcard are members of the South Wales Mounted Brigade of Despatch Riders and were stationed at Aylsham during the First World War from 1914 to 1915. The post office ceased to operate from these premises around 1934.

NOW: Over the years the building has been occupied by a number of businesses, including the International Stores in the late 1960s, Gateway supermarket for a few years and today Somerfields who have been there for the last ten years. Mr Roger Vail is the present store manager.

Post Office, Bacton-on-Sea. J 6648. (*Webster's Series.*)

THEN – BACTON POST OFFICE, *c.* **1920:** Bacton village post office was run by Mr George Webster from as early as 1904. He was in partnership with a Mr Haggith from 1905 onwards. During this time they were involved in grocery, drapers, a boot and shoe warehouse, fancy repository and methylated spirit vendors. This postcard was published by Mr Webster, who is probably the gentleman standing in the shop doorway. The post office closed around 1975.

NOW: The view today has drastically changed, with the post office completely demolished. The demolition took place around 1976, probably to make way for the widening of the coast road (B1159). This picture shows part of the site now being used as a car park for customers who visit the shops opposite. The buildings seen just above the car in the background seem to be the only original ones remaining, compared to our top picture.

THEN – BANNINGHAM POST OFFICE *c.* **1908:** The lady in the doorway could well be Mrs Harriet Harme, who was sub-postmistress at the time. The post office and village stores served the two villages of Colby and Banningham for 100 years, finally closing in 2000. Mrs Heather Townsend ran it for the last sixteen years and at the age of 23 she became the youngest postmistress in Norfolk, having taken over from the oldest – 92 years old Mrs Annie Daniels. Legend has it that Mrs Daniels arranged for her son's and husband's funerals in the lunch hour to avoid closing the post office, public service at its best!

NOW: The building is still owned by Mr and Mrs Townsend and has not changed a great deal. In 2000 they decided to convert it into a holiday cottage, with much of the work being done by themselves to a very high standard. This took longer than expected, but by 2007 the 'The Old Post Office' was ready for the next chapter in its history.

THEN – BARNHAM BROOM POST OFFICE, *c.* 1919: Barnham Broom post office was thought to have closed down between 1929 and 1935. The sub-postmaster at the time was Mr William John Pease. Since its closure it has been operated from a number of locations in the village. The present post office is still thriving, being located at the the crossroads in the centre of the village.

NOW: The building today has not changed a great deal. The old wooden gates have gone and gable roof windows have been installed, overall the property has been restored to a very high standard by the present owners, Mr and Mrs Reynolds, who have lived there since 1993.

THEN – BARTON BENDISH POST OFFICE *c.* **1905:** The post office cottages were built around 1713. Mr William Bailey was listed as being the first sub-postmaster in 1858 and he was followed by four generations of the Horn family who ran it from 1881 until 1965. Mr James Horn, sub-postmaster in 1904, was also the village blacksmith. The lady to the left of the picture is Mrs Polly Riches, in the centre doorway is Mrs Dora Horn and the young man far right is believed to be master Frederick Belham. The post office closed around 1967.

NOW: This must have been one of the very few thatched post offices in the county of Norfolk. The cottages have now been fully restored as can be seen by the beautifully thatched roof. The cottages are now privately owned by Albanwise Farming.

THEN – BEACHAMWELL POST OFFICE, *c.* **1900:** Mr Henry Rix was sub-postmaster when this picture was taken as can be seen on the board above the door. He was followed by Mrs Sarah Rix who was sub-postmistress in 1907, it was still in the Rix family in 1929. Following sub-postmasters were Mrs Copperswaite, Mr Grief and Mr and Mrs Pywell. The post office is still going today, but has been under threat of closure for some time.

NOW: Mrs Barbara Alexander has been sub-postmistress and shopkeeper since 1980. The shop was closed in 1998 due to the economic climate and the increase in competition from supermarkets coupled with two burglaries. Sadly it closed a week before this picture was taken, on the 19th May, 2009.

Post Office, Bintree Norfolk.

THEN – BINTREE POST OFFICE, *c.* 1929: At the time when this postcard was published, Mr George Farrow was sub-postmaster and cycle agent to the village of Bintree. Records show that Mr William Chapman was sub-postmaster around 1900. The Post Office finally closed on January 1st, 1965 with Mrs Sarah Farrow being the last sub-postmistress.

NOW: The building has changed completely with a really high standard of restoration having been carried out by the present owner, Mr Jim Riches. Like many others that are now privately-owned residences, it has not lost it connection to the past and is called 'The Old Post Office'.

Post Office, Brancaster. 10.

THEN – BRANCASTER POST OFFICE, *c.* **1950:** It is believed that the building started life as stabling for horses. In 1904 Mr John William Blackburn was village grocer and sub-postmaster, over the years there were various other owners, including Mr Samuel John Jacobs who was librarian and sub-postmaster in 1929. The last owners were Mrs Merle Johnson (postmistress) and Mr Harry Johnson (baker) who moved into the shop next door around 1955.

NOW: Long gone are the advertising signs that adorned the outer walls and the board displaying postcards for sale. The building has not changed a great deal and was converted into private holiday cottages sometime in the 1980s. Today there is still a post office in Brancaster, recently moved from the grocery shop to the Simms Reeve Institute in January 2008.

Burnham Thorpe.

THEN – BURNHAM THORPE POST OFFICE *c.* **1905:** This postcard shows an idyllic scene of small children and a gentleman on a motorcycle. The two ladies in the doorway may well be the spinster sisters, Winnie and Alice Huggins whose father, Mr Fred Muggins was the local blacksmith. The post office closed around 1935 with the the building eventually being demolished.

NOW: The present building, which is built on the same site, is set back approximately 30ft further from the road than its predecessor. This carried on trading as a post office and shop until it finally closed around 1977. For a short time it was run from the Nelson Public House. The property is now a private residence known as 'The Old Post Office'.

THEN – CAWSTON POST OFFICE, *c.* 1910: Mr Samuel Joseph Forster was sub-postmaster in 1904 and general grocer and agent for Gilby Ltd., wine and spirit merchant. He was followed by Mr Frederick William Moulton who was also sub-postmaster and grocer in 1929. Cawston closed as a post office in 1974, at that time it was run by Mr Sid Grey, who was manager for a company which operated under the name of Barwells. The post office was then transferred to its present location in the village.

NOW: Mr and Mrs Des Cook bought the shop and ran it as a general store up until 2004, after which it was sold on to a property developer who converted the premises into two cottages. In comparing the two pictures we can see that the motor car has certainly made its mark since 1910.

THEN – CLEY POST OFFICE, *c.* **1920:** This post office is located almost in the centre of Cley on a busy narrow coast road through the village. In 1900 Mr Edward Hudson was recorded as being the sub-postmaster. Mr Weedon was the last sub-postmaster and with his wife ran the post office and shop for 33½ years. After the loss of Mr Weedon, Mrs. Weedon carried on for a short time in a building further down the street. This finally closed at Christmas 2003.

NOW: After closing as a post office and shop, the building became a Tea-room, a Bakery, and at one time a Vegetarian Restaurant. Today it is a privately-owned dwelling and long gone are those wonderful old advertising signs of Cadburys Chocolate, Seaside Rock for Sale and Lamberts Cocoa Essence, which once adorned the windows.

THEN – COCKLEY CLEY POST OFFICE, *c.* 1916: This postcard shows the post office as it appeared around the time of the 1914–18 First World War. The poster, which can be seen to the left of the chimney, reads: 'RECRUITS ARE NOW WANTED FOR ALL BRANCHES OF HIS MAJESTY'S ARMY – GOD SAVE THE KING'. As usual everything has stopped for the photographer, including the Royal Mail cart, horse and postman. Past sub-postmasters included Miss Mary Ann Wegg (1900), Mr Arthur Root (1904). It finally closed in 1949 with Mrs A. Butters being the last sub-postmistress.

NOW: It would have been very hard to locate this post office without the help of some of the villagers. It has been completely demolished. The bungalow pictured, now occupies the approximate site where the post office was. It is now the private dwelling of Mr And Mrs Betty Chivers, who have been living there for the past 18 years in a location known as 'Riverside'.

THEN – ERPINGHAM POST OFFICE, *c.* 1910: Letters from Norwich arrived by cart at 6am and 2.30pm for callers only. The sub-postmaster was Mr Benjamin Barstard who was also the local carpenter and wheelwright. The nearest money order and telegraph office was at Hanworth. This one was the second post office in Erpingham.

NOW: The post office has been completely demolished, and the site is now occupied by a private house, owned by Mr T Amis (grandson of Mrs Amis – the last sub-postmistress). Further down in the same street, the very first post office is still standing in the form of a pretty, privately-owned, thatched cottage.

THEN – BRIDGE STREET POST OFFICE, FAKENHAM, *c.* 1907: Moved from Old Post Office Street in 1906, it was in the hands of Mr Thomas Earnest Pengelley. Mr Pengelley is the gentleman wearing a bowler hat, standing by the front of the Royal Mail van. In 1933 it was moved to the junction of Holt Road and Queen's Road. This heralded the end of a Crown Post Office in Fakenham.

NOW: The magnificent metal balustrade and the name of Fakenham above the shop are long-since gone The building is home to Estate Agents Helton Duffey and still retains much of its old charm and character. For many years it was the local office of the of the *Dereham and Fakenham Times* and *Eastern Daily Press*.

THEN – OLD POST OFFICE STREET, FAKENHAM, *c.* 1906: The post office was first run on a sub-post office basis around 1871 by Mr Martin Bembridge, who died in 1895. Mr Thomas Earnest Pengelley succeeded him as postmaster and Fakenham established its first Crown Post Office. Moving later to Bridge Street in 1906, where a sub-post office had previously been.

NOW: Having for many years been the local showrooms and works of the Eastern Electricity Board, the building is now the offices of a long-established Fakenham firm of solicitors – Butcher Andrews. The building presents a rather different look today, with the arched windows having been removed.

THEN – WELLS ROAD POST OFFICE, FAKENHAM *c.* **1971:** Wells road post office was originally built for military use during the First World War. Over the years it has been home to a number of businesses, including Mr Norman Woodhouse (signwriter), Mr Spencer (sub-postmaster), Mr Steward (cobbler), and Fakenham Electrical, who occupied the left-hand side. The building was demolished in 1971 and new shops and offices were erected in the same year. Mr Collison was sub-postmaster for two and a half years and continued as such in the new self-service shop.

NOW: Pearl River Take-Away is now in the shop where Fakenham Electrical used to be. The right-hand side is now Corders Budgens of Fakenham store, under the ownership of Mr And Mrs Corder. For a short period of time the new building and old post office were both standing together. The old post office wood buildings have now made way for a car park at the front. Sadly the post office closed on 12th August, 2008. The shop has been completely updated by the present owners to a very high standard and, although it has lost the post office, it remains one of Fakenham's busiest shops.

THEN – FIELD DALLING POST OFFICE, *c.* **1919:** This picture postcard was posted at Field Dalling on 24th April, 1919. Mr J W Seppings was grocer and sub-postmaster at the time. Other sub-postmasters were Mr Roberts (1977), Mr Ringer (1989). By the end of the 1990s the village grocery shop and post office had both closed down.

NOW: Like other villages in Norfolk, Field Dalling has had a slow decline in amenities. The Primary school closed in 1977 followed by the public house in 1986. Long gone are the enamel signs advertising 'Cadburys Cocoa' and 'Sunlight Soap'. The building is now a privately-owned dwelling. According to the 2001 census, Field Dalling had a population of around 273.

THEN – GARVESTONE POST OFFICE, *c.* **1917:** One of the earliest recorded sub-postmasters was a Mr Matthew Finch (1900). Garvestone post office was first closed in 1939 as the Post Master in Norwich did not think that the facility was needed because there was another post office in Thuxton. A new shopkeeper in Garvestone, Mrs Kathleen Kiddle, backed by the Parish Council applied for another post office in 1940. The application was successful and it opened later that year. It was run by Mrs Kiddle until 2002 when she had to retire through ill health. It was then carried on by Mrs Jane Aldridge assisted by Mrs Joy Nichols until it closed on 14th October, 2003.

NOW: The post office building, like so many others, has now become a privately-owned dwelling. Garvestone at this moment in time is not entirely without a post office. In December 2003 Mrs Jane Aldridge started to run it from the Village Hall two mornings a week.

THEN – GREAT SNORING POST OFFICE, *c.* **1945:** Great Snoring village is approximately seven miles inland from Wells-next-the-Sea. In the past, the village had two public houses, three shops, a blacksmith and carpenter. Mr Henry Green was the village sub-postmaster and carpenter in 1904. In 1929, Mr Thomas Styman was recorded as being sub-postmaster, and he was succeeded by his son John. The shop and post office finally closed in April 1984.

NOW: The shop and double-fronted windows have been removed in keeping with the rest of the building. A feature has been made where the letterbox once was and this now privately-owned residence still makes a very attractive picture with its old flint walls.

Post Office, Great Witchingham.   *Lenwade.*

THEN – GREAT WITCHINGHAM POST OFFICE, *c.* 1914: This post office is situated on a very busy road, the A1067 to Norwich. The buildings attached to the right have had a few changes made to them over the years, but the main post office building is still the same. One of the earliest sub-postmasters was Mr George E Harvey (1900). Later postmasters that followed were a Mr Howard, Mr Symes, Mr Hedge and Mr.and Mrs Lumbard.

NOW: Great Witchingham Post Office is still going strong today. It was taken over by Mr and Mrs A S Patrick on 31st March, 1999. In this latest picture the present owners can be seen standing in the shop doorway.

THEN – GRESSENHALL POST OFFICE, *c.* 1910: The post office in Gressenhall is situated on the corner of the village green in this very attractive Norfolk village. One of the earliest recorded sub-postmistresses was Miss Ella Pleasance Tye in 1903, who was also the village grocer and draper. Other sub-postmasters who later followed on were Mr Godfrey and Mr and Mrs Hinds.

NOW: The building has not changed much and is a very busy shop still serving the people of Gressenhall today. The post office and grocery shop is now run by Mr and Mrs Chisholm who have been there since 2004 and can be seen standing together in front of their shop.

THEN – GUIST POST OFFICE, *c.* 1937: Improvements were made to the village by Sir Thomas Cook, including a new Post Office which was built on the site of the old one and was set further back from the road. The old post office was demolished in 1928 and in January 1929 the new one was opened. The sub-postmaster at the time was Mr T C W Vincent, who was later succeeded by his son, Mr C T C Vincent. The flags decorating the front were possibly celebrating the 1937 George VI Jubilee.

NOW: The building remains much the same today, apart from the wall at the front being demolished to make way for off-road parking. After the Vincent family retired it changed hands two more times before Mr B Avery took over as the present sub-postmaster. He has been at the helm since 1988.

THEN – GUNTHORPE POST OFFICE, *c.* **1913:** Mrs Margaret Kidd was sub-postmistress and can be seen standing in the first doorway. The postman is believed to be Mr Clitheroe from Melton Constable. Miss Laura Kidd was grocer and sub-postmistress in 1929, with various other owners following. Finally closing around 1973, the last owners being the Bond family. After closing it was moved to a council house and run by Mrs Fincham and then by Mrs Pippa Bunting from her garage, which was later turned into a post office for approximately 12 years.

NOW: With the post-box in the wall missing, and one or two other small alterations to door and window positions, it can still be easily identified from the old picture and is now a private dwelling. The restoration work has been carried out to a high standard, allowing the building to blend in with other properties in the village.

THEN – HEMPTON GREEN POST OFFICE AND STORES, *c.* **1908:** The sub-postmaster in 1908 was Mr Edward John Fennings. Towards the end of the First World War the shop and post office came under the ownership of Mr William Albert Utting, being the first of three generations, followed by Mr Charles Albert Utting and finally Mr William Utting. It ceased to be a sub-post office in 1972 and Mr William Utting continued running the shop until his retirement in 1977.

NOW: The premises today have not changed a great deal and still retains its old-world charm of bygone days. Since 1994 it has been an exclusive ladies fashion shop under the name of 'Elizabeth Darby'.

Post Office, High Kelling.

113229

THEN – HIGH KELLING POST OFFICE, *c.* 1935: Mrs Sarah Harper opened this post office on Bryan Bullen's Corner in 1930 and it closed around 1935. It is believed that the business was then carried on by a Mr and Mrs Denmark from a bungalow (Mr Denmark being a postman at the time) prior to the post office moving to its present site. As can be seen from the picture, the post office building and yard was once used for the stabling of horses.

NOW: A shop was opened on this site and served teas outside for visitors to the Sanatorium. It was expanded by a Mr Goudge in the 1950s to become a post office. The present sub-postmistress is Jan Kemp who took over in 2001. The original building was knocked down and a new one rebuilt with a spacious car park at the front for customers who frequent this busy shop and post office today.

THEN – HINDOLVESTON POST OFFICE, *c.* **1909:** Hindolveston post office was first situated in the shop attached to the village bakery. At its height this was a major local business consisting of a mill, the bakery and the baker's house. The sails of the mill ceased to work around 1925, though milling, powered by a diesel engine, continued for some years later. The last loaf of bread was baked in 1957 and the post office and shop closed in 1971. The baker's house and post office seen in the picture dates back to 1740. Past postmasters and owners were: Mrs Agnes Bowman, Mr Orris Pegg, Mr Davidson, Mr Faulkner and Mr College.

NOW: The old post office is now a private dwelling. A few alterations externally have been made which adds to the charm and character of the building. The mill, which was part of the bakery business, is still standing at the rear of the premises. Today the house is called 'The Old Bakery'.

THEN – INGWORTH POST OFFICE, *c.* 1969: The sub-postmaster of the first post office in Ingworth village was Mr James Gaul (1900). Later it was taken over by Mr John and Mrs Maggie Amis, who ran the business for forty-two years. Upon retiring they handed the business over to their grand-daughter, Mrs Win Bastard and her husband Vic, who had the business for more than thirty years, finally retiring at the age of 73 in 1991 when the post office and shop closed. Pictured are Mrs Win Bastard (left) with friends.

NOW: With the post office and shop long gone the cottage has been changed back to a private dwelling under the ownership of Mr Tony and Mrs Gill Chambers, who have been there since 1992.

THEN – LANGHAM POST OFFICE, *c.* **1914:** Known as 'Wizards End' Post Office within the village of Langham. The building dates from early 18th century and was the only post office in England to have a blue post-box set into the wall. Past sub-postmasters were Mr Elijah William Boast (1900), Mr Greenlands and Mr S E Mullender. The last sub-postmaster was Mr David Butcher, who with his wife Linda, ran the post office from July, 1984 until it finally closed on October 31st, 2004 – which happened to be Hallow'een night, a fitting connection to Wizards End post office.

NOW: Not having changed a great deal apart from the pointed arched woodwork above the door which was demolished during the Second World War by a rather speedy lady ambulance driver from nearby Langham airfield. This was later replaced only to be demolished a second time by the same lady a few days later! The blue post-box set in the wall is still there today. The property is now the private residence of Mr and Mrs Butcher who can be seen standing in front of this delightful old building. The 'Wizards End' sign above the door is the original sign and was kindly displayed by Mr Butcher for our picture.

THEN – LITCHAM POST OFFICE, *c.* **1911:** This picture shows the building when Mr W A Warnes was sub-postmaster, who took over sometime between 1909 and 1911 from Mr Oliver Charles Chapman. The post office was relocated to another part of the village due to a fire, but later returned to its present site and, to date, still operates as a post office.

NOW: The post office was moved back to its original premises in 1948 (the three dormer roof windows having been removed) when Mr Gordon Bailey was made sub-postmaster until his retirement in 1986. There were various other occupants until 1995 when Mr and Mrs J M Troup took over and are currently running the post office, grocery shop and off-licence.

THEN – LITTLE DUNHAM POST OFFICE *c.* **1920:** Situated in the very picturesque village of Little Dunham, this post office was once run by a Mr Say who also had a garage business opposite. One of the earliest recorded sub-postmasters was Mr George Goodman (1900). Mr Alvin Coughlin was the last sub-postmaster who ran the business for 12 years until it closed in 1993. As you can see from the goods on display, it was once a very busy shop and post office in days gone by.

NOW: The shop front has now been removed and the door to the right has been taken out, and it has been restored to a very high standard as a private dwelling by Mr Paul Hoft and Joanne Whitlock who have been the owners since 2000.

POST OFFICE. MARHAM. 6.

THEN – MARHAM POST OFFICE, *c.* 1902: This postcard has everything that today's serious postcard collector requires, a shop front, the Royal Mail pony and trap, a three-wheel bicycle, postmen and customers. The sub-postmaster at the time was Mr Robert Parlett who was also a grocer, draper, cobbler and newsagent. The post office closed around 1929 but was run as a grocery shop by Mrs Amelia Jane Parlett until it closed completely in 1947.

NOW: The building is now the privately-owned residence of Mrs King. The old stables to the right of the picture is where Mr Parlett had the cobbler's shop. Today the stable building has been converted into a thriving hairdressing business under the name of 'Shirley's Hairdressers' owned and run by Mrs King's daughter.

THEN – MELTON CONSTABLE POST OFFICE, *c.* **1909:** Situated on the corner of Gordon Road, Mr John Linder was sub-postmaster in 1904. During and after the First World War, Miss Nellie Linder was at the helm, a lady with a reputation for speaking her mind. This postcard portrays a rather nice connection to the past with the postman wearing their American civil war type caps.

NOW: The shop front has completely changed and is now a high-class butchers' shop. M & M Rutland was established in 1972 at another premises in Gordon Road, moving to the old Post Office building in 1986. The family-run business, which includes three daughters and one son, recently won the coveted *Eastern Daily Press* 'Norfolk Foods Awards' for butcher of the year, sponsored by Easton College.

THEN – NARBOROUGH POST OFFICE, *c.* 1912: Mr John George Faulkner was grocer, draper and sub-postmaster. The cottages adjoining the post office were known as Rattle Row, later simply as The Row or Post Office Row (cottage rents at this time were two shillings per week). Most of the cottages in The Row were occupied by the workforce of Vynne & Everett Ltd, maltsters and dealers in oil cake, coal, corn and general merchandise etc. Sadly Post Office Row was demolished around the 1950s.

NOW: The site is occupied by a large privately-owned bungalow. The post office was situated roughly to the right half of the present building, with the main part of Post Office Row to the left-hand side. Today it is very hard to imagine that the old Post Office and cottages ever existed.

POST OFFICE STREET, NORTH ELMHAM.

THEN – NORTH ELMHAM POST OFFICE AND VILLAGE STORES, *c.* **1906:** North Elmham Post Office was for a number of years owned by the Kerrison family. In 1904, Robert Kerrison was the owner and traded as family grocer, draper, ironmonger, dealer in ammunition and sub-postmaster. Mr Kerrison finally sold it around 1969. The shop and post office continued under one, or two, other proprietors and ceased trading as a grocer's in 2003.

NOW: As you enter the shop, to the left you will see that North Elmham still has a busy Post Office. The main part of the premises are occupied by Steers Estate Agents situated in a pleasant spacious area – both under the ownership of Mr J Steer.

THEN – NORTH WALSHAM POST OFFICE, c. 1908: This grand old building in King's Arms Street was the town hall until on August 27th, 1899, when it was destroyed by fire. Mr John Dixon, local builder and auctioneer, rebuilt it in 1901 as the Manor Hotel. In 1900 it became the post office with Mr George Rolf as postmaster, it finally closed in 1966.

NOW: The building is still the same today. The plaque on the front which reads 'YE OLD TOWN HALL HOUSE 1901' is still there and it is now home to the local Employment Exchange or Job Centre as it is sometimes referred to.

THEN – REEPHAM POST OFFICE *c.* **1906:** The original post office was on this side of the market place from around 1850. The post was driven off every night to Norwich and incoming post brought to Reepham at 6.00am the following morning by a pony and red-painted trap. This picture was taken when Mr and Mrs Rudd were sub-postmasters. From left to right are: Mr Maurice Mole, Mr Herbert Rudd (sub-postmaster), Mr William Alford (the elder), Miss Elsie Hall (daughter of John Hall, local harnessmaker), Mr William Alford (the younger), Donald Chapman (future sub-postmaster). The post office finally closed around the 1930s.

NOW: This part of Reepham has not changed a great deal over the years. In the past the premises have been occupied by a number of different businesses, a sweet shop and cycle repairs run by Mr Harry Franklin for around eight years, and a children's wear shop known as 'Young and Beautiful' for a short time. The present occupier is Mr Geoff Deal who took over in 1985 and has a very well stocked fruit, vegetable and florist shop under the delightful name of 'Meloncaulie Rose'.

THEN – SAXLINGHAM NETHERGATE POST OFFICE *c.* **1909:** A busy scene outside the post office in 1909. This postcard was addressed to a Miss Ruby Cole of the Cycle Depot, Mulbarton, and sent from Saxlingham. The sub-postmaster at the time was Mr Horace George Simmons who was followed on by other members of the Simmons family into the business. Saxlingham is believed to have had a post office from as early as 1837. The post office closed around 1974.

NOW: Today the building, which used to be three separate dwellings including the post office on the far left of the picture, is now one large cottage, privately owned by Mr M F Pye.

THEN – SAXTHORPE POST OFFICE, *c.* **1937:** Mrs Hilda White (née Harrison) was sub-postmistress for 56 years after taking over from her grandfather in 1942. During the time she ran the business, Hilda only had two days off, one to attend a Royal Garden Party and the other one was for a day out at the Royal Norfolk Show. Our picture shows Hilda when she was about 12 years old. The post office closed in January 1999, Hilda having turned 82 when she finally retired.

NOW: The property still remains in the family and has been handed down to Mrs Hilda White's grandson, Mr Justin Friar, who took over on 7th October, 2004. The building is currently being restored as a private dwelling and we can expect a high standard as Mr Friar specialises in property renovation. Like so many others it will possibly be known as 'The Old Post Office'.

POST OFFICE, SCULTHORPE.

No. J. & S. 7169

THEN – SCULTHORPE POST OFFICE, *c.* 1914: This postcard is post marked 20th August, 1914, and was published by Mrs W P Sewter who was sub-postmistress and owner of the general store in the Street, Sculthorpe. Standing in the shop doorway is Mrs W P Sewter and her daughter, Hannah Bessie Sewter. Mr William Parke Sewter was founder of the post office and stores and is recorded as being sub-postmaster as far back as 1900.

NOW: It would not be too hard to find this building today as there is no change to the front or structure of it. The Post Office is now a privately-owned house and the shop front has been carefully restored to a high standard.

THEN – SOUTH CREAKE POST OFFICE, *c.* **1904:** South Creake is approximately 6 miles south-west of Fakenham. This postcard show Cartwright's Village Stores and Post Office, which is overlooking the village green. It was first owned by the Cartwrights in the early 1800s and since then has changed hands within and outside the family. Llewellyn Cartwright owned it in 1904, Mrs Sarah Cartwright in 1929. In 1936, it was sold to Mr Alex Seaman, and then to a Mr Watts-Russell, eventually returning back to the Seaman family in 1994. In 2000 it changed hands once again.

NOW: Set back on the west side of South Creake village green and having been fully restored to a very high standard, the former Post Office is now four holiday cottages: *Cornloft Cottage*, *Cornloft Lodge*, *Seascape Cottage* and *Cranberry Cottage* – all fitting names to this lovely old building.

THEN – SWAFFHAM POST OFFICE, *c.* **1916:** Swaffham Post Office was built in 1894. One of the earliest recorded sub-postmasters was Mr Henry Titlow (1900). The building is quite distinctive with its cone-shaped turret. One interesting story about the adjoining shop, namely 'Howard's Sadlers', was that Mr Howard and his son used to rescue buckets that had fallen into wells – they even rescued a guest who fell 160ft into a well behind the Angel Inn, and survived! The post office eventually closed in 1968, which coincided with a new one opening on the opposite side of the road in the same year.

NOW: Today the building has not changed too much. The date depicting when it was built is still over the doorway, as is the wording 'Post Office' above the front windows which have been changed over the years. It is now a very busy pet food shop called 'Heads and Tails' under the ownership of Mr and Mrs Garner, who have been there since 1994.

THEN – TATTERSETT POST OFFICE, *c.* **1904:** Another building which has not changed much over the years and is located on a very quiet back road off the busy A148 to King's Lynn. When this picture was taken, Mrs Sarah Ann Walker was sub-postmistress and shopkeeper. In 1929 Mrs Ethel Sands was sub-postmistress, and she can be seen standing in the doorway. The nearest money-order and telegraph office was located in East Rudham.

NOW: Like many other village post offices it was finally closed, around the mid 1930s it is believed, and became a private dwelling. The property is still owned by the Sands' family, with Mr and Mrs Michael Sands seen standing in the same doorway over 70 years later. Mr Michael Sands is grandson to the late Mr and Mrs Ethel Sands.

THEN – THURSFORD POST OFFICE, *c.* **1904:** Mr Allen Bertie Stedman was sub-postmaster when this picture was taken. The grocery, drapery and post office was run by Mr and Mrs Pointer from 1929 when they first married. The grocery and drapery side of the business eventually finished and the post office continued after Mrs Pointer handed it over to her daughter, Mrs Joan Allen, who operated it from the 1970s until its closure in the early 1980s.

NOW: Mrs Allen recalls the story of a red flag being placed outside the post office so that Dr Sturdy, who used to travel through the village each day, would call in to see Mrs Pointer and she would tell him which household in the village needed a visit. How times have changed! Like so many other old post offices in Norfolk the building has undergone some alterations, one being the removal of the shop front. It is now a privately-owned dwelling.

THEN – TITTLESHALL POST OFFICE, *c.* **1904:** The shopkeeper and staff gather to have their photograph taken in front of a well-stocked shop. There was certainly no shortage of shoes for the people of Tittleshall judging by the amount hanging from the shop front. This card captures the relaxed pace of village life in the early 1900s. The post office closed around the mid 1980s. The Ostrich public house sign can clearly be seen in the background.

NOW: The building has had the shop front removed and has been very tastefully restored. The house is now privately-owned by Mr and Mrs Richardson. Note the post-box, possibly the original, which can still be seen in between the four windows at the far end.

THEN – WEASENHAM POST OFFICE, *c.* **1910:** Mr Thomas Livermore Deadman was sub-postmaster in 1904 and was later succeeded by his son Mr Max Deadman. They were followed by Mr Frank Andrews, Mr Turnbull, Colonel Phayer, Mr Hewitt and finally Mr Merrett. Postman and postmistress who worked the area were Mr Edgar Abbs (All Saints round) and Miss Daphne Smalley (Weasenham St Peter with Wellingham round). It finally closed around 1993.

NOW: The main part of the house has not changed. The shop and post office part to the right has been transformed into an attached bungalow with views facing Weasenham's picturesque village green and pond. Both properties are privately owned.

THEN – WELLS POST OFFICE, *c.* **1915:** Built in 1912 and opened in 1913 it replaced the old post office which was in Staithe Street, where the last sub-postmaster was Miss Jane Southgate (1905). Station Road Post Office was the first main general post office in Wells and at the time employed around 20 staff. Our picture shows the 1915 staff with 2 telegram boys seated at the front. The picture has not changed much, with the exception that the bicycles will have now been replaced by cars. I cannot imagine the staff being photographed in the same position today!

NOW: Today the Wells Post Office is still going strong, although the number of staff have been considerably reduced in size. Mrs Carol Starkey is now the present sub-postmistress and runs the operation with the help of 2 staff and 6 postmen.

THEN – WEST DEREHAM POST OFFICE, *c.* **1928:** The village of West Dereham is situated approximately 4 miles south-east of Downham Market. One of the first recorded sub-postmasters was Mr Edward E Barrow. At the time this postcard was published the sub-postmaster was Mr Edward Willimont. Closing down around 1958 the last sub-postmaster being a Mr Douglas.

NOW: The house and old post office is much the same with the exception that the shop front has now been changed to look more like part of the house. The metal railings are still there and it is believed that they were removed during the war and replaced by a wood fence so as not to be used for war effort metal. After the war the metal fence mysteriously reappeared. The property is now a private dwelling belonging to Mr and Mrs Miles.

THEN – WEYBOURNE POST OFFICE, *c.* 1920: The post office was located approximately in the centre of the pretty north Norfolk village of Weybourne. Mr George David John Spink was sub-postmaster around 1900. He was also an earthenware dealer, furniture broker, provison merchant, ironmonger, draper and general grocer. It closed as a post office in the early 1920s.

NOW: The old post office is now a private dwelling, although the post office side of the business moved to the existing premises in the same road, it carried on as a sweet and grocery shop and at one time an antique shop until it eventually closed. One or two alterations have been made over the years, but as can be seen it still retains its charm and character.

THEN – WITTON BRIDGE POST OFFICE, *c.* **1904:** One of the earliest recorded sub-postmasters was Mr Charles Cole (1890) who was also shopkeeper and pork butcher. Mr George Sidney Savage was next to carry on the business from 1937. The last owner was a Mr Beechcroft with the shop and post office being managed by Mr Charles and Sally Owles and Mrs London. The post office and shop finally closed in June, 1988.

NOW: The buildings today have not altered too much. Most of the dwellings in the street are now privately owned. This small village shop appeared to be very busy in 1904 and was probably used a great deal by locals and the large number of people who lived in the surrounding countryside.

THEN – WOOD DALLING POST OFFICE, *c.* **1904:** Mrs Elizabeth Churchman was post-mistress when this picture was taken. Mr William Gaskin and his wife Ada bought the post office and stores in 1933 from Mrs Churchman, and they ran it until 1962 when their son Leslie and his wife Sheila took over and continued the business until their retirement in 2001.

NOW: Fortunately the post office is still in existence today, being operated by Mr Joice who continued after Mr and Mrs Gaskin retired. Mr Joice runs both the postal side of the business and the grocery shop.

Post Office Wood Norton

THEN – WOOD NORTON POST OFFICE, *c.* **1921:** This post office was run by Mr Frederick Bidewell from 1904 to 1929, after 1929 Mr Charles Edward Mason became sub-postmaster. The last sub-postmistress was Hetty Smith who operated the post office with her husband Archie until he died. It closed in the mid 1960s but was then carried on by Mrs Smith in a building opposite until she died, we believe in the mid-1990s.

NOW: This is now a private dwelling called 'The Old Post Office' owned by Mr and Mrs C Holland. The building is set back from a lovely village green which we are told is getting smaller due to the large vehicles travelling through.

208. POST OFFICE, WORSTEAD

THEN – WORSTEAD POST OFFICE, *c.* **1935:** The earliest recorded sub-postmistresses were Mary Ann and Elizabeth Dyball in 1836. Other sub-postmasters were James Benjamin Copping, 1904, and Wilfred Bristow, 1929. The business was sold to a Mrs Mable Flowerday Hunn in 1946. It finally closed around 1977 and moved further down the road.

NOW: The present sub-postmistress is Allison Henderson who has operated the business since it moved from the above location. The old post office is now a privately-owned dwelling.

LOCAL TITLES PUBLISHED BY JOHN NICKALLS PUBLICATIONS

A Garland of Waveney Valley Tales
A compilation of illustrated tales from Suffolk of yesteryear.

A Level Country
Sketches of its Fenland folk.

A Pharmacist's Tale
The joys and delights encountered preserving pharmacy history.

A Shepherd and his Flock
Fifty years with Suffolk sheep.

Curiosities of Norfolk
A county guide to the unusual.

Curiosities of Suffolk
A county guide to the unusual.

Great Ouse Country
Sketches of its riverside folk and history from source to mouth.

Great Yarmouth & Gorleston: Then and Now
A pictorial tour in old postcards and modern-day photographs.

Harwich, Dovercourt & Parkeston, Vol 3
Selection of old picture postcards.

Harwich, Dovercourt & Parkeston: Then and Now
A pictorial tour in old postcards and modern-day photographs.

In and Around Norwich: Then and Now
Another look at Norwich.

Melton Constable, Briston & District, Book 1
A portrait in old picture postcards.

Melton Constable, Briston & District, Book 2
A further portrait in postcards.

Nature Trails in Northamptonshire
A series of illustrated walks.

Newmarket, Town and Turf
A pictorial tour.

Norfolk Dialect and its Friends
Ten years of FOND memories

North Norfolk
A portrait in old picture postcards.

North Norfolk: The Heritage Coast
Timeless scenes through the lens.

Norwich: Then and Now
A pictorial tour in old postcards and modern-day photographs.

Norwich: Then and Now
A third selection of old picture postcards.

Robber Barons and Fighting Bishops
Norman influence in East Anglia.

Shires, Sales and Pigs
The story of an Ely Auctioneers. George Comins, 1856–1997.

Suffolk's Lifeboats
In postcards and photographs.

S'Wonderful
A symphony of musical memories.

'Smarvellous
More musical memories.

Tipple & Teashop Rambles in Northamptonshire
A series of illustrated walks.

Walks in the Wilds of Cambridgeshire
A series of illustrated walks.

Wicken: a Fen Village
A third selection of old pictures.